DATE DUE

FE 26 '93			
MY 19 '95			
AU 15 '02			
MY 11 '06			

BOOKS BY MARK STRAND

MARK
STRAND
SELECTED
POEMS

MARK
STRAND
SELECTED
POEMS

Alfred A. Knopf   New York
1991

THIS IS A BORZOI BOOK
PUBLISHED BY ALFRED A. KNOPF, INC.

Library of Congress Cataloging-in-Publication Data

Strand, Mark
  [Poems. Selections]
  Selected poems / Mark Strand.—1st Knopf ed.
    p.   cm.
  ISBN 0-679-73301-9
  I. Title.
  PS3569.T69A6   1990   90-4902
  811'.54—dc20   CIP

Manufactured in the United States of America
Published October 15, 1990
Reprinted Four Times
Sixth Printing, October 1991

TO JULES AND JESS

CONTENTS

From SLEEPING WITH ONE EYE OPEN (1964)

From REASONS FOR MOVING (1968)

From DARKER (*1970*)

From THE STORY OF OUR LIVES (*1973*)

From THE LATE HOUR (1978)

NEW POEMS (1980)

Sleeping with One Eye Open

Sleeping with One Eye Open

Unmoved by what the wind does,
The windows
Are not rattled, nor do the various
Areas
Of the house make their usual racket—
Creak at
The joints, trusses and studs.
Instead,
They are still. And the maples,
Able
At times to raise havoc,
Evoke
Not a sound from their branches
Clutches.
It's my night to be rattled,
Saddled
With spooks. Even the half-moon
(Half man,
Half dark) , on the horizon,
Lies on
Its side casting a fishy light
Which alights
On my floor, lavishly lording
Its morbid
Look over me. Oh, I feel dead,
Folded
Away in my blankets for good, and
Forgotten.
My room is clammy and cold,
Moonhandled
And weird. The shivers
Wash over
Me, shaking my bones, my loose ends
Loosen,

And I lie sleeping with one eye open,
Hoping
That nothing, nothing will happen.

When the Vacation Is Over for Good

It will be strange
Knowing at last it couldn't go on forever,
The certain voice telling us over and over
That nothing would change,

And remembering too,
Because by then it will all be done with, the way
Things were, and how we had wasted time as though
There was nothing to do,

When, in a flash
The weather turned, and the lofty air became
Unbearably heavy, the wind strikingly dumb
And our cities like ash,

And knowing also,
What we never suspected, that it was something like summer
At its most august except that the nights were warmer
And the clouds seemed to glow,

And even then,
Because we will not have changed much, wondering what
Will become of things, and who will be left to do it
All over again,

And somehow trying,
But still unable, to know just what it was
That went so completely wrong, or why it is
We are dying.

Violent Storm

Those who have chosen to pass the night
Entertaining friends
And intimate ideas in the bright,
Commodious rooms of dreams
Will not feel the slightest tremor
Or be wakened by what seems
Only a quirk in the dry run
Of conventional weather. For them,
The long night sweeping over these trees
And houses will have been no more than one
In a series whose end
Only the nervous or morbid consider.
But for us, the wide-awake, who tend
To believe the worst is always waiting
Around the next corner or hiding in the dry,
Unsteady branch of a sick tree, debating
Whether or not to fell the passerby,
It has a sinister air.
How we wish we were sunning ourselves
In a world of familiar views
And fixed conditions, confined
By what we know, and able to refuse
Entry to the unaccounted for. For now,
Deeper and darker than ever, the night unveils
Its dubious plans, and the rain
Beats down in gales
Against the roof. We sit behind
Closed windows, bolted doors,
Unsure and ill at ease
While the loose, untidy wind,
Making an almost human sound, pours
Through the open chambers of the trees.
We cannot take ourselves or what belongs
To us for granted. No longer the exclusive,

Last resorts in which we could unwind,
Lounging in easy chairs,
Recalling the various wrongs
We had been done or spared, our rooms
Seem suddenly mixed up in our affairs.
We do not feel protected
By the walls, nor can we hide
Before the duplicating presence
Of their mirrors, pretending we are the ones who stare
From the other side, collected
In the glassy air.
A cold we never knew invades our bones.
We shake as though the storm were going to hurl us down
Against the flat stones
Of our lives. All other nights
Seem pale compared to this, and the brilliant rise
Of morning after morning seems unthinkable.
Already now the lights
That shared our wakefulness are dimming
And the dark brushes against our eyes.

Old People On the Nursing Home Porch

Able at last to stop
And recall the days it took
To get them here, they sit
On the porch in rockers
Letting the faded light
Of afternoon carry them off

I see them moving back
And forth over the dullness
Of the past, covering ground
They did not know was there,
And ending up with nothing
Save what might have been.

And so they sit, gazing
Out between the trees
Until in all that vacant
Wash of sky, the wasted
Vision of each one
Comes down to earth again.

It is too late to travel
Or even find a reason
To make it seem worthwhile.
Already now, the evening
Reaches out to take
The aging world away.

And soon the dark will come,
And these tired elders feel
The need to go indoors
Where each will lie alone
In the deep and sheepless
Pastures of a long sleep.

Taking a Walk with You

Lacking the wit and depth
That inform our dreams'
Bright landscapes,
This countryside
Through which we walk
Is no less beautiful
For being only what it seems.
Rising from the dyed
Pool of its shade,
The tree we lean against
Was never made to stand
For something else,
Let alone ourselves.
Nor were these fields
And gullies planned
With us in mind.
We live unsettled lives
And stay in a place
Only long enough to find
We don't belong.
Even the clouds, forming
Noiselessly overhead,
Are cloudy without
Resembling us and, storming
The vacant air,
Don't take into account
Our present loneliness.
And yet, why should we care?
Already we are walking off
As if to say,
We are not here,
We've always been away.

Keeping Things Whole

In a field
I am the absence
of field.
This is
always the case.
Wherever I am
I am what is missing.

When I walk
I part the air
and always
the air moves in
to fill the spaces
where my body's been.

We all have reasons
for moving.
I move
to keep things whole.

The Whole Story

*—I'd rather you didn't feel it neces-
sary to tell him, "That's a fire. And
what's more, we can't do anything
about it, because we're on this
train, see?"*

How it should happen this way
I am not sure, but you
Are sitting next to me,
Minding your own business
When all of a sudden I see
A fire out the window.

I nudge you and say,
"That's a fire. And what's more,
We can't do anything about it,
Because we're on this train, see?"
You give me an odd look
As though I had said too much.

But for all you know I may
Have a passion for fires,
And travel by train to keep
From having to put them out.
It may be that trains
Can kindle a love of fire.

I might even suspect
That you are a fireman
In disguise. And then again
I might be wrong. Maybe
You are the one
Who loves a good fire. Who knows?

Perhaps you are elsewhere,
Deciding that with no place
To go you should not
Take a train. And I,
Seeing my own face in the window,
May have lied about the fire.

The Tunnel

A man has been standing
in front of my house
for days. I peek at him
from the living room
window and at night,
unable to sleep,
I shine my flashlight
down on the lawn.
He is always there.

After a while
I open the front door
just a crack and order
him out of my yard.
He narrows his eyes
and moans. I slam
the door and dash back
to the kitchen, then up
to the bedroom, then down.

I weep like a schoolgirl
and make obscene gestures
through the window. I
write large suicide notes
and place them so he
can read them easily.
I destroy the living
room furniture to prove
I own nothing of value.

When he seems unmoved
I decide to dig a tunnel
to a neighboring yard.
I seal the basement off
from the upstairs with
a brick wall. I dig hard
and in no time the tunnel
is done. Leaving my pick
and shovel below,

I come out in front of a house
and stand there too tired to
move or even speak, hoping
someone will help me.
I feel I'm being watched
and sometimes I hear
a man's voice,
but nothing is done
and I have been waiting for days.

Poem

He sneaks in the backdoor,
tiptoes through the kitchen,
the living room, the hall,
climbs the stairs and enters
the bedroom. He leans
over my bed and says he has come
to kill me. The job
will be done in stages.

First, my toenails
will be clipped, then my toes
and so on until
nothing is left of me.
He takes a small instrument
from his keychain and begins.
I hear Swan Lake being played
on a neighbor's hifi and start to hum.

How much time passes,
I cannot tell. But when I come to
I hear him say he has reached my neck
and will not be able to continue
because he is tired. I tell him
that he has done enough,
that he should go home and rest.
He thanks me and leaves.

I am always amazed at
how easily satisfied
some people are.

Make Believe Ballroom Time

Judging from his suit which was excessively
drab but expensive, and his speech which was
uninflected and precise, I guessed he was a
banker, perhaps a lawyer, even a professor in
one of the larger, better universities. It never
occurred to me that he might be something
else until, during a lull in our conversation,
he suddenly got up and began dancing. The
others at the party, plainly disturbed by this,
affected a more intense involvement in their
conversations than was necessary. They spoke
loudly, rapidly. But the man continued danc-
ing. And because I recognized what calling,
what distant music he obeyed, I envied him.

Reasons for Moving

The Mailman

It is midnight.
He comes up the walk
and knocks at the door.
I rush to greet him.
He stands there weeping,
shaking a letter at me.
He tells me it contains
terrible personal news.
He falls to his knees.
"Forgive me! Forgive me!" he pleads.

I ask him inside.
He wipes his eyes.
His dark blue suit
is like an inkstain
on my crimson couch.
Helpless, nervous, small,
he curls up like a ball
and sleeps while I compose
more letters to myself
in the same vein:

"You shall live
by inflicting pain.
You shall forgive."

The Accident

A train runs over me.
I feel sorry
for the engineer
who crouches down
and whispers in my ear
that he is innocent.

He wipes my forehead,
blows the ashes
from my lips.
My blood steams
in the evening air,
clouding his glasses.

He whispers in my ear
the details of his life—
he has a wife
and child he loves,
he's always been
an engineer.

He talks
until the beam
from someone's flashlight
turns us white.
He stands.
He shakes his jacket out

and starts to run.
The cinders crack
under his boots,
the air is cold
and thick
against his cheeks.

Back home he sits
in the kitchen,
staring at the dark.
His face is flushed,
his hands are pressed
between his knees.

He sees me sprawled
and motionless
beside the tracks
and the faint blooms
of my breath
being swept away;

the fields bend
under the heavy sheets
of the wind
and birds scatter
into the rafters
of the trees.

He rushes
from the house,
lifts the wreckage
of my body in his arms
and brings me back.
I lie in bed.

He puts his head
down next to mine
and tells me
that I'll be all right.
A pale light
shines in his eyes.

I listen to the wind
press hard against the house.
I cannot sleep.
I cannot stay awake.
The shutters bang.
The end of my life begins.

The Man in the Tree

I sat in the cold limbs of a tree.
I wore no clothes and the wind was blowing.
You stood below in a heavy coat,
the coat you are wearing.

And when you opened it, baring your chest,
white moths flew out, and whatever you said
at that moment fell quietly onto the ground,
the ground at your feet.

Snow floated down from the clouds into my ears.
The moths from your coat flew into the snow.
And the wind as it moved under my arms, under my chin,
whined like a child.

I shall never know why
our lives took a turn for the worse, nor will you.
Clouds sank into my arms and my arms rose.
They are rising now.

I sway in the white air of winter
and the starling's cry lies down on my skin.
A field of ferns covers my glasses; I wipe them away
in order to see you.

I turn and the tree turns with me.
Things are not only themselves in this light.
You close your eyes and your coat
falls from your shoulders,

the tree withdraws like a hand,
the wind fits into my breath, yet nothing is certain.
The poem that has stolen these words from my mouth
may not be this poem.

The Man in the Mirror

for Decio de Souza

I walk down the narrow,
carpeted hall.
The house is set.
The carnation in my buttonhole

precedes me like a small
continuous explosion.
The mirror
is in the living room.

You are there.
Your face is white, unsmiling, swollen.
The fallen body of your hair
is dull and out of place.

Buried in the darkness of your pockets,
your hands are motionless.
You do not seem awake.
Your skin sleeps

and your eyes lie in the deep
blue of their sockets,
impossible to reach.
How long will all this take?

I remember how we used to stand
wishing the glass
would dissolve between us,
and how we watched our words

cloud that bland,
innocent surface,
and when our faces blurred
how scared we were.

But that was another life.
One day you turned away
and left me here
to founder in the stillness of your wake.

Your suit floating, your hair
moving like eel grass
in a shallow bay, you drifted
out of the mirror's room, through the hall

and into the open air.
You seemed to rise and fall
with the wind, the sway
taking you always farther away, farther away.

Darkness filled your sleeves.
The stars moved through you.
The vague music of your shrieking
blossomed in my ears.

I tried forgetting what I saw;
I got down on the floor,
pretending to be dead.
It did not work.

My heart bunched in my rib-cage like a bat,
blind and cowardly,
beating in and out,
a solemn, irreducible black.

The things you drove me to!
I walked in the calm of the house,
calling you back.
You did not answer.

I sat in a chair
and stared across the room.
The walls were bare.
The mirror was nothing without you.

I lay down on the couch
and closed my eyes.
My thoughts rose in the dark
like faint balloons,

and I would turn them over
one by one and watch them shiver.
I always fell into a deep
and arid sleep.

Then out of nowhere late one night
you reappeared,
a huge vegetable moon,
a bruise coated with light.

You stood before me,
dreamlike and obscene,
your face lost
under layers of heavy skin,

your body sunk in a green
and wrinkled sea of clothing.
I tried to help you
but you refused.

Days passed
and I would rest
my cheek against the glass,
wanting nothing but the old you.

I sang so sadly
that the neighbors wept
and dogs whined with pity.
Some things I wish I could forget.

You didn't care,
standing still while flies
collected in your hair
and dust fell like a screen before your eyes.

You never spoke
or tried to come up close.
Why did I want so badly
to get through to you?

It still goes on.
I go into the living room and you are there.
You drift in a pool
of silver air

where wounds and dreams of wounds
rise from the deep
humus of sleep
to bloom like flowers against the glass.

I look at you
and see myself
under the surface.
A dark and private weather

settles down on everything.
It is colder
and the dreams wither away.
You stand

like a shade
in the painless glass,
frail, distant, older
than ever.

It will always be this way.
I stand here scared
that you will disappear,
scared that you will stay.

The Last Bus

(*Rio de Janeiro, 1966*)

It is dark.
A slight rain
dampens the streets.
Nothing moves

in Lota's park.
The palms hang
over the matted grass,
and the voluminous bushes,

bundled in sheets,
billow beside the walks.
The world is out of reach.
The ghosts of bathers rise

slowly out of the surf and turn
high in the spray.
They walk on the beach
and their eyes burn

like stars.
And Rio sleeps:
the sea is a dream
in which it dies and is reborn.

The bus speeds.
A violet cloud
unravels in its wake.
My legs begin to shake.

My lungs fill up with steam.
Sweat covers my face
and falls to my chest.
My neck and shoulders ache.

Not even sure
that I am awake,
I grip the hot
edge of the seat.

The driver smiles.
His pants are rolled above his knees
and his bare calves
gleam in the heat.

A woman tries to comfort me.
She puts her hand under my shirt
and writes the names of flowers
on my back.

Her skirt is black.
She has a tiny skull
and crossbones on each knee.
There is a garden in her eyes

where rows of dull,
white tombstones crowd the air
and people stand,
waving goodbye.

I have the feeling I am there.
She whispers through her teeth
and puts her lips
against my cheek.

The driver turns.
His eyes are closed and he is combing
back his hair.
He tells me to be brave.

I feel my heartbeat
growing fainter as he speaks.
The woman kisses me again.
Her jaw creaks

and her breath clings
to my neck like mist.
I turn to the window's
cracked pane

streaked with rain.
Where have I been?
I look toward Rio—
nothing is the same.

The Christ who stood
in a pool of electric light
high on his hill
is out of sight.

And the bay is black.
And the black city
sinks into its grave.
And I shall never come back.

The Ghost Ship

Through the crowded street
It floats,

Its vague
Tonnage like wind.

It glides
Through the sadness

Of slums
To the outlying fields.

Slowly,
Now by an ox,

Now by a windmill,
It moves.

Passing
At night like a dream

Of death,
It cannot be heard;

Under the stars
It steals.

Its crew
And passengers stare;

Whiter than bone,
Their eyes

Do not
Turn or close.

The Kite

for Bill and Sandy Bailey

It rises over the lake, the farms,
The edge of the woods,
And like a body without arms
Or legs it swings
Blind and blackening in the moonless air.
The wren, the vireo, the thrush
Make way. The rush
And flutter of wings
Fall through the dark
Like a mild rain.
We cover our heads and ponder
The farms and woods that rim
The central lake.
A barred owl sits on a limb
Silent as bark.
An almost invisible
Curtain of rain seems to come nearer.
The muffled crack and drum
Of distant thunder
Blunders against our ears.

A row of hills appears.
It sinks into a valley
Where farms and woods surround a lake.
There is no rain.
It is impossible to say what form
The weather will take.
We blow on our hands,
Trying to keep them warm,
Hoping it will not snow.
Birds fly overhead.
A man runs by
Holding the kite string.

He does not see us standing dark
And still as mourners under the sullen sky.
The wind cries in his lapels. Leaves fall
As he moves by them.
His breath blooms in the chill
And for a time it seems that small
White roses fill the air,
Although we are not sure.

Inside the room
The curtains fall like rain.
Darkness covers the flower-papered walls,
The furniture and floors,
Like a mild stain.
The mirrors are emptied, the doors
Quietly closed. The man, asleep
In the heavy arms of a chair,
Does not see us
Out in the freezing air
Of the dream he is having.
The beating of wings and the wind
Move through the deep,
Echoing valley. The kite
Rises over the lake,
The farms, the edge of the woods
Into the moonless night
And disappears.
And the man turns in his chair,
Slowly beginning to wake.

Moontan

for Donald Justice

The bluish, pale
face of the house
rises above me
like a wall of ice

and the distant,
solitary
barking of an owl
floats toward me.

I half close my eyes.

Over the damp
dark of the garden
flowers swing
back and forth
like small balloons.

The solemn trees,
each buried
in a cloud of leaves,
seem lost in sleep.

It is late.
I lie in the grass,
smoking,
feeling at ease,
pretending the end
will be like this.

Moonlight
falls on my flesh.
A breeze
circles my wrist.

I drift.
I shiver.
I know that soon
the day will come
to wash away the moon's
white stain,

that I shall walk
in the morning sun
invisible
as anyone.

What to Think Of

Think of the jungle,
The green steam rising.

It is yours.
You are the prince of Paraguay.

Your minions kneel
Deep in the shade of giant leaves

While you drive by
Benevolent as gold.

They kiss the air
That moments before

Swept over your skin,
And rise only after you've passed.

Think of yourself, almost a god,
Your hair on fire,

The bellows of your heart pumping.
Think of the bats

Rushing out of their caves
Like a dark wind to greet you;

Of the vast nocturnal cities
Of lightning bugs

Floating down
From Minas Gerais;

Of the coral snakes;
Of the crimson birds

With emerald beaks;
Of the tons and tons of morpho butterflies

Filling the air
Like the cold confetti of paradise.

The Marriage

The wind comes from opposite poles,
traveling slowly.

She turns in the deep air.
He walks in the clouds.

She readies herself,
shakes out her hair,

makes up her eyes,
smiles.

The sun warms her teeth,
the tip of her tongue moistens them.

He brushes the dust from his suit
and straightens his tie.

He smokes.
Soon they will meet.

The wind carries them closer.
They wave.

Closer, closer.
They embrace.

She is making a bed.
He is pulling off his pants.

They marry
and have a child.

The wind carries them off
in different directions.

The wind is strong, he thinks
as he straightens his tie.

I like this wind, she says
as she puts on her dress.

The wind unfolds.
The wind is everything to them.

The Babies

Let us save the babies.
Let us run downtown.
The babies are screaming.

You shall wear mink
and your hair shall be done.
I shall wear tails.

Let us save the babies
even if we run in rags
to the heart of town.

Let us not wait for tomorrow.
Let us drive into town
and save the babies.

Let us hurry.
They lie in a warehouse
with iron windows and iron doors.

The sunset pink of their skin
is beginning to glow.
Their teeth

poke through their gums
like tombstones.
Let us hurry.

They have fallen asleep.
Their dreams
are infecting them.

Let us hurry.
Their screams rise
from the warehouse chimney.

We must move faster.
The babies have grown into their suits.
They march all day in the sun without blinking.

Their leader sits in a bullet-proof car and applauds.
Smoke issues from his helmet.
We cannot see his face:

we are still running.
More babies than ever are locked in the warehouse.
Their screams are like sirens.

We are still running to the heart of town.
Our clothes are getting ragged.
We shall not wait for tomorrow.

The future is always beginning now.
The babies are growing into their suits.
Let us run to the heart of town.

Let us hurry.
Let us save the babies.
Let us try to save the babies.

Eating Poetry

Ink runs from the corners of my mouth.
There is no happiness like mine.
I have been eating poetry.

The librarian does not believe what she sees.
Her eyes are sad
and she walks with her hands in her dress.

The poems are gone.
The light is dim.
The dogs are on the basement stairs and coming up.

Their eyeballs roll,
their blond legs burn like brush.
The poor librarian begins to stamp her feet and weep.

She does not understand.
When I get on my knees and lick her hand,
she screams.

I am a new man.
I snarl at her and bark.
I romp with joy in the bookish dark.

The Dirty Hand

(*after Carlos Drummond de Andrade*)

My hand is dirty.
I must cut it off.
To wash it is pointless.
The water is putrid.
The soap is bad.
It won't lather.
The hand is dirty.
It's been dirty for years.

I used to keep it
out of sight,
in my pants pocket.
No one suspected a thing.
People came up to me,
wanting to shake hands.
I would refuse
and the hidden hand,
like a dark slug,
would leave its imprint
on my thigh.
And then I realized
it was the same
if I used it or not.
Disgust was the same.

How many nights
in the depths of the house
I washed that hand,
scrubbed it, polished it,
dreamed it would turn
to diamond or crystal
or even, at last,
into a plain white hand,

the clean hand of a man,
that you could shake,
or kiss, or hold
in one of those moments
when two people confess
without saying a word . . .
Only to have
the incurable hand,
lethargic and crablike,
open its dirty fingers.

And the dirt was vile.
It was not mud or soot
or the caked filth
of an old scab
or the sweat
of a laborer's shirt.
It was a sad dirt
made of sickness
and human anguish.
It was not black;
black is pure.
It was dull,
a dull grayish dirt.

It is impossible
to live with this
gross hand that lies
on the table.
Quick! Cut it off!
Chop it to pieces
and throw it
into the ocean.
With time, with hope
and its intricate workings
another hand will come,
pure, transparent as glass,
and fasten itself to my arm.

The Door

The door is before you again and the shrieking
Starts and the mad voice is saying here here.
The myth of comfort dies and the couch of her
Body turns to dust. Clouds enter your eyes.

It is autumn. People are jumping from jetliners;
Their relatives leap into the air to join them.
That is what the shrieking is about. Nobody wants
To leave, nobody wants to stay behind.

The door is before you and you are unable to speak.
Your breathing is slow and you peer through
The window. Your doctor is wearing a butcher's apron
And carries a knife. You approve.

And you remember the first time you came. The leaves
Spun from the maples as you ran to the house.
You ran as you always imagined you would.
Your hand is on the door. This is where you came in.

FROM

Darker

The New Poetry Handbook

for Greg Orr and Greg Simon

1   If a man understands a poem,
      he shall have troubles.

2   If a man lives with a poem,
      he shall die lonely.

3   If a man lives with two poems,
      he shall be unfaithful to one.

4   If a man conceives of a poem,
      he shall have one less child.

5   If a man conceives of two poems,
      he shall have two children less.

6   If a man wears a crown on his head as he writes,
      he shall be found out.

7   If a man wears no crown on his head as he writes,
      he shall deceive no one but himself.

8   If a man gets angry at a poem,
      he shall be scorned by men.

9   If a man continues to be angry at a poem,
      he shall be scorned by women.

10   If a man publicly denounces poetry,
       his shoes will fill with urine.

11   If a man gives up poetry for power,
       he shall have lots of power.

12   If a man brags about his poems,
        he shall be loved by fools.

13   If a man brags about his poems and loves fools,
        he shall write no more.

14   If a man craves attention because of his poems,
        he shall be like a jackass in moonlight.

15   If a man writes a poem and praises the poem of a
        fellow,
        he shall have a beautiful mistress.

16   If a man writes a poem and praises the poem of a
        fellow overly,
        he shall drive his mistress away.

17   If a man claims the poem of another,
        his heart shall double in size.

18   If a man lets his poems go naked,
        he shall fear death.

19   If a man fears death,
        he shall be saved by his poems.

20   If a man does not fear death,
        he may or may not be saved by his poems.

21   If a man finishes a poem,
        he shall bathe in the blank wake of his passion
        and be kissed by white paper.

The Remains

for Bill and Sandy Bailey

I empty myself of the names of others. I empty my pockets.
I empty my shoes and leave them beside the road.
At night I turn back the clocks;
I open the family album and look at myself as a boy.

What good does it do? The hours have done their job.
I say my own name. I say goodbye.
The words follow each other downwind.
I love my wife but send her away.

My parents rise out of their thrones
into the milky rooms of clouds. How can I sing?
Time tells me what I am. I change and I am the same.
I empty myself of my life and my life remains.

Giving Myself Up

I give up my eyes which are glass eggs.
I give up my tongue.
I give up my mouth which is the constant dream of my
    tongue.
I give up my throat which is the sleeve of my voice.
I give up my heart which is a burning apple.
I give up my lungs which are trees that have never seen the
    moon.
I give up my smell which is that of a stone traveling through
    rain.
I give up my hands which are ten wishes.
I give up my arms which have wanted to leave me anyway.
I give up my legs which are lovers only at night.
I give up my buttocks which are the moons of childhood.
I give up my penis which whispers encouragement to my
    thighs.
I give up my clothes which are walls that blow in the wind
and I give up the ghost that lives in them.
I give up. I give up.
And you will have none of it because already I am beginning
again without anything.

The Room

It is an old story, the way it happens
sometimes in winter, sometimes not.
The listener falls to sleep,
the doors to the closets of his unhappiness open

and into his room the misfortunes come—
death by daybreak, death by nightfall,
their wooden wings bruising the air,
their shadows the spilled milk the world cries over.

There is a need for surprise endings;
the green field where cows burn like newsprint,
where the farmer sits and stares,
where nothing, when it happens, is never terrible enough.

Letter

for Richard Howard

Men are running across a field,
pens fall from their pockets.
People out walking will pick them up.
It is one of the ways letters are written.

How things fall to others!
The self no longer belonging to me, but asleep
in a stranger's shadow, now clothing
the stranger, now leading him off.

It is noon as I write to you.
Someone's life has come into my hands.
The sun whitens the buildings.
It is all I have. I give it all to you. Yours,

Nostalgia

for Donald Justice

The professors of English have taken their gowns
to the laundry, have taken themselves to the fields.
Dreams of motion circle the Persian rug in a room you were in.
On the beach the sadness of gramophones
deepens the ocean's folding and falling.
It is yesterday. It is still yesterday.

Tomorrow

Your best friend is gone,
your other friend, too.
Now the dream that used to turn in your sleep,
sails into the year's coldest night.

What did you say?
Or was it something you did?
It makes no difference—the house of breath collapsing
around your voice, your voice burning, are nothing to worry
    about.

Tomorrow your friends will come back;
your moist open mouth will bloom in the glass of storefronts.
Yes. Yes. Tomorrow they will come back and you
will invent an ending that comes out right.

The Dress

Lie down on the bright hill
with the moon's hand on your cheek,
your flesh deep in the white folds of your dress,
and you will not hear the passionate mole
extending the length of his darkness,
or the owl arranging all of the night,
which is his wisdom, or the poem
filling your pillow with its blue feathers.
But if you step out of your dress and move into the shade,
the mole will find you, so will the owl, and so will the poem,
and you will fall into another darkness, one you will find
yourself making and remaking until it is perfect.

The Guardian

The sun setting. The lawns on fire.
The lost day, the lost light.
Why do I love what fades?

You who left, who were leaving,
what dark rooms do you inhabit?
Guardian of my death,

preserve my absence. I am alive.

The Dance

The ghost of another comes to visit and we hold
communion while the light shines.
While the light shines, what else can we do?
And who doesn't have one foot in the grave?

I notice how the trees seem shaggy with leaves
and the steam of insects engulfs them.
The light falls like an anchor through the branches.
And which one of us is not being pulled down constantly?

My mind floats in the purple air of my skull.
I see myself dancing. I smile at everybody.
Slowly I dance out of the burning house of my head.
And who isn't borne again and again into heaven?

The Good Life

You stand at the window.
There is a glass cloud in the shape of a heart.
The wind's sighs are like caves in your speech.
You are the ghost in the tree outside.

The street is quiet.
The weather, like tomorrow, like your life,
is partially here, partially up in the air.
There is nothing you can do.

The good life gives no warning.
It weathers the climates of despair
and appears, on foot, unrecognized, offering nothing,
and you are there.

Black Maps

Not the attendance of stones,
nor the applauding wind,
shall let you know
you have arrived,

nor the sea that celebrates
only departures,
nor the mountains,
nor the dying cities.

Nothing will tell you
where you are.
Each moment is a place
you've never been.

You can walk
believing you cast
a light around you.
But how will you know?

The present is always dark.
Its maps are black,
rising from nothing,
describing,

in their slow ascent
into themselves,
their own voyage,
its emptiness,

the bleak, temperate
necessity of its completion.
As they rise into being
they are like breath.

And if they are studied at all
it is only to find,
too late, what you thought
were concerns of yours

do not exist.
Your house is not marked
on any of them,
nor are your friends,

waiting for you to appear,
nor are your enemies,
listing your faults.
Only you are there,

saying hello
to what you will be,
and the black grass
is holding up the black stars.

The Hill

I have come this far on my own legs,
missing the bus, missing taxis,
climbing always. One foot in front of the other,
that is the way I do it.

It does not bother me, the way the hill goes on.
Grass beside the road, a tree rattling
its black leaves. So what?
The longer I walk, the farther I am from everything.

One foot in front of the other. The hours pass.
One foot in front of the other. The years pass.
The colors of arrival fade.
That is the way I do it.

Coming to This

We have done what we wanted.
We have discarded dreams, preferring the heavy industry
of each other, and we have welcomed grief
and called ruin the impossible habit to break.

And now we are here.
The dinner is ready and we cannot eat.
The meat sits in the white lake of its dish.
The wine waits.

Coming to this
has its rewards: nothing is promised, nothing is taken away.
We have no heart or saving grace,
no place to go, no reason to remain.

Seven Poems

1   At the edge
of the body's night
ten moons are rising.

2   A scar remembers the wound.
The wound remembers the pain.
Once more you are crying.

3   When we walk in the sun
our shadows are like barges of silence.

4   My body lies down
and I hear my own
voice lying next to me.

5   The rock is pleasure
and it opens
and we enter it
as we enter ourselves
each night.

6   When I talk to the window
I say everything
is everything.

7   I have a key
so I open the door and walk in.
It is dark and I walk in.
It is darker and I walk in.

eep

There is the sleep of my tongue
speaking a language I can never remember—
words that enter the sleep of words
once they are spoken.

There is the sleep of one moment
inside the next, lengthening the night,
and the sleep of the window
turning the tall sleep of trees into glass.

The sleep of novels as they are read is soundless
like the sleep of dresses on the warm bodies of women.
And the sleep of thunder gathering dust on sunny days
and the sleep of ashes long after.

The sleep of wind has been known to fill the sky.
The long sleep of air locked in the lungs of the dead.
The sleep of a room with someone inside it.
Even the wooden sleep of the moon is possible.

And there is the sleep that demands I lie down
and be fitted to the dark that comes upon me
like another skin in which I shall never be found,
out of which I shall never appear.

Breath

When you see them
tell them I am still here,
that I stand on one leg while the other one dreams,
that this is the only way,

that the lies I tell them are different
from the lies I tell myself,
that by being both here and beyond
I am becoming a horizon,

that as the sun rises and sets I know my place,
that breath is what saves me,
that even the forced syllables of decline are breath,
that if the body is a coffin it is also a closet of breath,

that breath is a mirror clouded by words,
that breath is all that survives the cry for help
as it enters the stranger's ear
and stays long after the word is gone,

that breath is the beginning again, that from it
all resistance falls away, as meaning falls
away from life, or darkness falls from light,
that breath is what I give them when I send my love.

The Prediction

That night the moon drifted over the pond,
turning the water to milk, and under
the boughs of the trees, the blue trees,
a young woman walked, and for an instant

the future came to her:
rain falling on her husband's grave, rain falling
on the lawns of her children, her own mouth
filling with cold air, strangers moving into her house,

a man in her room writing a poem, the moon drifting into it,
a woman strolling under its trees, thinking of death,
thinking of him thinking of her, and the wind rising
and taking the moon and leaving the paper dark.

The One Song

I prefer to sit all day
like a sack in a chair
and to lie all night
like a stone in my bed.

When food comes
I open my mouth.
When sleep comes
I close my eyes.

My body sings
only one song;
the wind turns
gray in my arms.

Flowers bloom.
Flowers die.
More is less.
I long for more.

From a Litany

There is an open field I lie down in a hole I once dug and I praise the sky.
I praise the clouds that are like lungs of light.
I praise the owl that wants to inhabit me and the hawk that does not.
I praise the mouse's fury, the wolf's consideration.
I praise the dog that lives in the household of people and shall never be one of them.
I praise the whale that lives under the cold blankets of salt.
I praise the formations of squid, the domes of meandra.
I praise the secrecy of doors, the openness of windows.
I praise the depth of closets.
I praise the wind, the rising generations of air.
I praise the trees on whose branches shall sit the Cock of Portugal and the Polish Cock.
I praise the palm trees of Rio and those that shall grow in London.
I praise the gardeners, the worms and the small plants that praise each other.
I praise the sweet berries of Georgetown, Maine and the song of the white-throated sparrow.
I praise the poets of Waverly Place and Eleventh Street, and the one whose bones turn to dark emeralds when he stands upright in the wind.
I praise the clocks for which I grow old in a day and young in a day.
I praise all manner of shade, that which I see and that which I do not.
I praise all roofs from the watery roof of the pond to the slate roof of the customs house.
I praise those who have made of their bodies final embassies of flesh.
I praise the failure of those with ambition, the authors of leaflets and notebooks of nothing.

I praise the moon for suffering men.
I praise the sun its tributes.
I praise the pain of revival and the bliss of decline.
I praise all for nothing because there is no price.
I praise myself for the way I have with a shovel and I praise
    the shovel.
I praise the motive of praise by which I shall be reborn.
I praise the morning whose sun is upon me.
I praise the evening whose son I am.

My Life

The huge doll of my body
refuses to rise.
I am the toy of women.
My mother

would prop me up for her friends.
"Talk, talk," she would beg.
I moved my mouth
but words did not come.

My wife took me down from the shelf.
I lay in her arms. "We suffer
the sickness of self," she would whisper.
And I lay there dumb.

Now my daughter
gives me a plastic nurser
filled with water.
"You are my real baby," she says.

Poor child!
I look into the brown
mirrors of her eyes
and see myself

diminishing, sinking down
to a depth she does not know is there.
Out of breath,
I will not rise again.

I grow into my death.
My life is small
and getting smaller. The world is green.
Nothing is all.

My Death

Sadness, of course, and confusion.
The relatives gathered at the graveside,
talking about the waste, and the weather mounting,
the rain moving in vague pillars offshore.

This is Prince Edward Island.
I came back to my birthplace to announce my death.
I said I would ride full gallop into the sea
and not look back. People were furious.

I told them about attempts I had made in the past,
how I starved in order to be the size of Lucille,
whom I loved, to inhabit the cold space
her body had taken. They were shocked.

I went on about the time
I dove in a perfect arc that filled
with the sunshine of farewell and I fell
head over shoulders into the river's thigh.

And about the time
I stood naked in the snow, pointing a pistol
between my eyes, and how when I fired my head bloomed
into health. Soon I was alone.

Now I lie in the box
of my making while the weather
builds and the mourners shake their heads as if
to write or to die, I did not have to do either.

"The Dreadful Has Already Happened"

The relatives are leaning over, staring expectantly.
They moisten their lips with their tongues. I can feel
them urging me on. I hold the baby in the air.
Heaps of broken bottles glitter in the sun.

A small band is playing old fashioned marches.
My mother is keeping time by stamping her foot.
My father is kissing a woman who keeps waving
to somebody else. There are palm trees.

The hills are spotted with orange flamboyants and tall
billowy clouds move behind them. "Go on, Boy,"
I hear somebody say, "Go on."
I keep wondering if it will rain.

The sky darkens. There is thunder.
"Break his legs," says one of my aunts,
"Now give him a kiss." I do what I'm told.
The trees bend in the bleak tropical wind.

The baby did not scream, but I remember that sigh
when I reached inside for his tiny lungs and shook them
out in the air for the flies. The relatives cheered.
It was about that time I gave up.

Now, when I answer the phone, his lips
are in the receiver; when I sleep, his hair is gathered
around a familiar face on the pillow; wherever I search
I find his feet. He is what is left of my life.

My Life By Somebody Else

I have done what I could but you avoid me.
I left a bowl of milk on the desk to tempt you.
Nothing happened. I left my wallet there, full of money.
You must have hated me for that. You never came.

I sat at my typewriter naked, hoping you would wrestle me
to the floor. I played with myself just to arouse you.
Boredom drove me to sleep. I offered you my wife.
I sat her on the desk and spread her legs. I waited.

The days drag on. The exhausted light falls like a bandage
over my eyes. Is it because I am ugly? Was anyone
ever so sad? It is pointless to slash my wrists. My hands
would fall off. And then what hope would I have?

Why do you never come? Must I have you by being
somebody else? Must I write *My Life* by somebody else?
My Death by somebody else? Are you listening?
Somebody else has arrived. Somebody else is writing.

Elegy 1969

(after Carlos Drummond de Andrade)

You slave away into your old age
and nothing you do adds up to much.
Day after day you go through the same motions,
you shiver in bed, you get hungry, you want a woman.

Heroes standing for lives of sacrifice and obedience
fill the parks through which you walk.
At night in the fog they open their bronze umbrellas
or else withdraw to the empty lobbies of movie houses.

You love the night for its power of annihilating,
but while you sleep, your problems will not let you die.
Waking only proves the existence of The Great Machine
and the hard light falls on your shoulders.

You walk among the dead and talk
about times to come and matters of the spirit.
Literature wasted your best hours of love-making.
Weekends were lost, cleaning your apartment.

You are quick to confess your failure and to postpone
collective joy to the next century. You accept
rain, war, unemployment and the unjust distribution of wealth
because you can't, all by yourself, blow up Manhattan Island.

Courtship

There is a girl you like so you tell her
your penis is big, but that you cannot get yourself
to use it. Its demands are ridiculous, you say,
even self-defeating, but to be honored somehow,
briefly, inconspicuously in the dark.

When she closes her eyes in horror,
you take it all back. You tell her you're almost
a girl yourself and can understand why she is shocked.
When she is about to walk away, you tell her
you have no penis, that you don't

know what got into you. You get on your knees.
She suddenly bends down to kiss your shoulder and you know
you're on the right track. You tell her you want
to bear children and that is why you seem confused.
You wrinkle your brow and curse the day you were born.

She tries to calm you, but you lose control.
You reach for her panties and beg forgiveness as you do.
She squirms and you howl like a wolf. Your craving
seems monumental. You know you will have her.
Taken by storm, she is the girl you will marry.

Not Dying

These wrinkles are nothing.
These gray hairs are nothing.
This stomach which sags
with old food, these bruised
and swollen ankles,
my darkening brain,
they are nothing.
I am the same boy
my mother used to kiss.

The years change nothing.
On windless summer nights
I feel those kisses
slide from her dark
lips far away,
and in winter they float
over the frozen pines
and arrive covered with snow.
They keep me young.

My passion for milk
is uncontrollable still.
I am driven by innocence.
From bed to chair I crawl
and back again.
I shall not die.
The grave result
and token of birth, my body
remembers and holds fast.

The Way It Is

The world is ugly.
And the people are sad.
WALLACE STEVENS

I lie in bed.
I toss all night
in the cold unruffled deep
of my sheets and cannot sleep.

My neighbor marches in his room,
wearing the sleek
mask of a hawk with a large beak.
He stands by the window. A violet plume

rises from his helmet's dome.
The moon's light
spills over him like milk and the wind rinses the white
glass bowls of his eyes.

His helmet in a shopping bag,
he sits in the park, waving a small American flag.
He cannot be heard as he moves
behind trees and hedges,

always at the frayed edges
of town, pulling a gun on someone like me. I crouch
under the kitchen table, telling myself
I am a dog, who would kill a dog?

My neighbor's wife comes home.
She walks into the living room,
takes off her clothes, her hair falls down her back.
She seems to wade

through long flat rivers of shade.
The soles of her feet are black.
She kisses her husband's neck
and puts her hands inside his pants.

My neighbors dance.
They roll on the floor, his tongue
is in her ear, his lungs
reek with the swill and weather of hell.

Out on the street people are lying down
with their knees in the air, tears
fill their eyes, ashes
enter their ears.

Their clothes are torn
from their backs. Their faces are worn.
Horsemen are riding around them, telling them why
they should die.

My neighbor's wife calls to me, her mouth is pressed
against the wall behind my bed.
She says, "My husband's dead."
I turn over on my side,

hoping she has not lied.
The walls and ceiling of my room are gray—
the moon's color through the windows of a laundromat.
I close my eyes.

I see myself float
on the dead sea of my bed, falling away,
calling for help, but the vague scream
sticks in my throat.

I see myself in the park
on horseback, surrounded by dark,
leading the armies of peace.
The iron legs of the horse do not bend.

I drop the reins. Where will the turmoil end?
Fleets of taxis stall
in the fog, passengers fall
asleep. Gas pours

from a tri-colored stack.
Locking their doors,
people from offices huddle together,
telling the same story over and over.

Everyone who has sold himself wants to buy himself back.
Nothing is done. The night
eats into their limbs
like a blight.

Everything dims.
The future is not what it used to be.
The graves are ready. The dead
shall inherit the dead.

FROM

The Story of Our Lives

Elegy for My Father

(*Robert Strand 1908 – 68*)

1   THE EMPTY BODY

The hands were yours, the arms were yours,
But you were not there.
The eyes were yours, but they were closed and would not open.
The distant sun was there.
The moon poised on the hill's white shoulder was there.
The wind on Bedford Basin was there.
The pale green light of winter was there.
Your mouth was there,
But you were not there.
When somebody spoke, there was no answer.
Clouds came down
And buried the buildings along the water,
And the water was silent.
The gulls stared.
The years, the hours, that would not find you
Turned in the wrists of others.
There was no pain. It had gone.
There were no secrets. There was nothing to say.
The shade scattered its ashes.
The body was yours, but you were not there.
The air shivered against its skin.
The dark leaned into its eyes.
But you were not there.

2   ANSWERS

Why did you travel?
Because the house was cold.
Why did you travel?
Because it is what I have always done between sunset and
*   sunrise.*

What did you wear?
I wore a blue suit, a white shirt, yellow tie, and yellow socks.
What did you wear?
I wore nothing. A scarf of pain kept me warm.
Who did you sleep with?
I slept with a different woman each night.
Who did you sleep with?
I slept alone. I have always slept alone.
Why did you lie to me?
I always thought I told the truth.
Why did you lie to me?
Because the truth lies like nothing else and I love the truth.
Why are you going?
Because nothing means much to me anymore.
Why are you going?
I don't know. I have never known.
How long shall I wait for you?
Do not wait for me. I am tired and I want to lie down.
Are you tired and do you want to lie down?
Yes, I am tired and I want to lie down.

3   YOUR DYING

Nothing could stop you.
Not the best day. Not the quiet. Not the ocean rocking.
You went on with your dying.
Not the trees
Under which you walked, not the trees that shaded you.
Not the doctor
Who warned you, the white-haired young doctor who saved
     you once.
You went on with your dying.
Nothing could stop you. Not your son. Not your daughter
Who fed you and made you into a child again.
Not your son who thought you would live forever.
Not the wind that shook your lapels.
Not the stillness that offered itself to your motion.

Not your shoes that grew heavier.
Not your eyes that refused to look ahead.
Nothing could stop you.
You sat in your room and stared at the city
And went on with your dying.
You went to work and let the cold enter your clothes.
You let blood seep into your socks.
Your face turned white.
Your voice cracked in two.
You leaned on your cane.
But nothing could stop you.
Not your friends who gave you advice.
Not your son. Not your daughter who watched you grow small.
Not fatigue that lived in your sighs.
Not your lungs that would fill with water.
Not your sleeves that carried the pain of your arms.
Nothing could stop you.
You went on with your dying.
When you played with children you went on with your dying.
When you sat down to eat,
When you woke up at night, wet with tears, your body sobbing,
You went on with your dying.
Nothing could stop you.
Not the past.
Not the future with its good weather.
Not the view from your window, the view of the graveyard.
Not the city. Not the terrible city with its wooden buildings.
Not defeat. Not success.
You did nothing but go on with your dying.
You put your watch to your ear.
You felt yourself slipping.
You lay on the bed.
You folded your arms over your chest and you dreamed of the
    world without you,
Of the space under the trees,
Of the space in your room,
Of the spaces that would now be empty of you,
And you went on with your dying.

Nothing could stop you.
Not your breathing. Not your life.
Not the life you wanted.
Not the life you had.
Nothing could stop you.

4 YOUR SHADOW

You have your shadow.
The places where you were have given it back.
The hallways and bare lawns of the orphanage have given it
    back.
The Newsboys Home has given it back.
The streets of New York have given it back and so have the
    streets of Montreal.
The rooms in Belém where lizards would snap at mosquitos
    have given it back.
The dark streets of Manaus and the damp streets of Rio have
    given it back.
Mexico City where you wanted to leave it has given it back.
And Halifax where the harbor would wash its hands of you has
    given it back.
You have your shadow.
When you traveled the white wake of your going sent your
    shadow below, but when you arrived it was there to greet
    you. You had your shadow.
The doorways you entered lifted your shadow from you and
    when you went out, gave it back. You had your shadow.
Even when you forgot your shadow, you found it again; it had
    been with you.
Once in the country the shade of a tree covered your shadow
    and you were not known.
Once in the country you thought your shadow had been cast
    by somebody else. Your shadow said nothing.
Your clothes carried your shadow inside; when you took them
    off, it spread like the dark of your past.
And your words that float like leaves in an air that is lost, in a
    place no one knows, gave you back your shadow.

Your friends gave you back your shadow.
Your enemies gave you back your shadow. They said it was
    heavy and would cover your grave.
When you died your shadow slept at the mouth of the furnace
    and ate ashes for bread.
It rejoiced among ruins.
It watched while others slept.
It shone like crystal among the tombs.
It composed itself like air.
It wanted to be like snow on water.
It wanted to be nothing, but that was not possible.
It came to my house.
It sat on my shoulders.
Your shadow is yours. I told it so. I said it was yours.
I have carried it with me too long. I give it back.

5   MOURNING

They mourn for you.
When you rise at midnight,
And the dew glitters on the stone of your cheeks,
They mourn for you.
They lead you back into the empty house.
They carry the chairs and tables inside.
They sit you down and teach you to breathe.
And your breath burns,
It burns the pine box and the ashes fall like sunlight.
They give you a book and tell you to read.
They listen and their eyes fill with tears.
The women stroke your fingers.
They comb the yellow back into your hair.
They shave the frost from your beard.
They knead your thighs.
They dress you in fine clothes.
They rub your hands to keep them warm.
They feed you. They offer you money.
They get on their knees and beg you not to die.

When you rise at midnight they mourn for you.
They close their eyes and whisper your name over and over.
But they cannot drag the buried light from your veins.
They cannot reach your dreams.
Old man, there is no way.
Rise and keep rising, it does no good.
They mourn for you the way they can.

6 THE NEW YEAR

It is winter and the new year.
Nobody knows you.
Away from the stars, from the rain of light,
You lie under the weather of stones.
There is no thread to lead you back.
Your friends doze in the dark
Of pleasure and cannot remember.
Nobody knows you. You are the neighbor of nothing.
You do not see the rain falling and the man walking away,
The soiled wind blowing its ashes across the city.
You do not see the sun dragging the moon like an echo.
You do not see the bruised heart go up in flames,
The skulls of the innocent turn into smoke.
You do not see the scars of plenty, the eyes without light.
It is over. It is winter and the new year.
The meek are hauling their skins into heaven.
The hopeless are suffering the cold with those who have
    nothing to hide.
It is over and nobody knows you.
There is starlight drifting on the black water.
There are stones in the sea no one has seen.
There is a shore and people are waiting.
And nothing comes back.
Because it is over.
Because there is silence instead of a name.
Because it is winter and the new year.

In Celebration

You sit in a chair, touched by nothing, feeling
the old self become the older self, imagining
only the patience of water, the boredom of stone.
You think that silence is the extra page,
you think that nothing is good or bad, not even
the darkness that fills the house while you sit watching
it happen. You've seen it happen before. Your friends
move past the window, their faces soiled with regret.
You want to wave but cannot raise your hand.
You sit in a chair. You turn to the nightshade spreading
a poisonous net around the house. You taste
the honey of absence. It is the same wherever
you are, the same if the voice rots before
the body, or the body rots before the voice.
You know that desire leads only to sorrow, that sorrow
leads to achievement which leads to emptiness.
You know that this is different, that this
is the celebration, the only celebration,
that by giving yourself over to nothing,
you shall be healed. You know there is joy in feeling
your lungs prepare themselves for an ashen future,
so you wait, you stare and you wait, and the dust settles
and the miraculous hours of childhood wander in darkness.

She

for Bill and Sandy Bailey

She slept without the usual concerns,
the troubling dreams—the pets
moving through the museum,
the carved monsters, the candles
giving themselves up to darkness.
She slept without caring what she looked like,
without considering the woman
who would come or the men who would leave
or the mirrors or the basin of cold water.
She slept on one side, the sheets
pouring into the room's cold air,
the pillow shapeless, her flesh
no longer familiar. Her sleep
was a form of neglect.
She did nothing for days,
the sun and moon had washed up
on the same shore. Her negligee
became her flesh, her flesh became
the soft folding of air over the sheets.
And there was no night, nor any sign of it.
Nothing curled in the air
but the sound of nothing,
the hymn of nothing, the humming
of the room, of its past.
Her flesh turned from itself
into the sheets of light.
She began to wake; her hair spilled
into the rivers of shadow.
Her eyes half-open, she saw the man across the room,
she watched him and could not choose
between sleep and wakefulness.
And he watched her
and the moment became their lives
so that she would never rise or turn from him,
so that he would always be there.

The Room

I stand at the back of a room
and you have just entered.
I feel the dust
fall from the air
onto my cheeks.
I feel the ice
of sunlight on the walls.
The trees outside
remind me of something
you are not yet aware of.
You have just entered.
There is something like sorrow
in the room.
I believe you think
it has wings
and will change me.
The room is so large
I wonder what you are thinking
or why you have come.
I ask you,
What are you doing?
You have just entered
and cannot hear me.
Where did you buy
the black coat you are wearing?
You told me once.
I cannot remember
what happened between us.
I am here. Can you see me?
I shall lay my words on the table
as if they were gloves,
as if nothing had happened.
I hear the wind
and I wonder what are

the blessings
born of enclosure.
The need to get away?
The desire to arrive?
I am so far away
I seem to be in the room's past
and so much here
the room is beginning
to vanish around me.
It will be yours soon.
You have just entered.
I feel myself drifting,
beginning to be
somewhere else.
Houses are rising
out of my past,
people are walking
under the trees.
You do not see them.
You have just entered.
The room is long.
There is a table in the middle.
You will walk
toward the table,
toward the flowers,
toward the presence of sorrow
which has begun to move
among objects,
its wings beating
to the sound of your heart.
You shall come closer
and I shall begin to turn away.
The black coat you are wearing,
where did you get it?
You told me once
and I cannot remember.
I stand at the back
of the room and I know

if you close your eyes
you will know why
you are here.
Soon you will take off your coat.
Soon the room's whiteness
will be a skin for your body.
I feel the turning of breath
around what we are going to say.
I know by the way
you raise your hand
you have noticed the flowers
on the table.
They will lie
in the wake of our motions
and the room's map
will lie before us
like a simple rug.
You have just entered.
There is nothing to be done.
I stand at the back of the room
and I believe you see me.
The light consumes the chair,
absorbing its vacancy,
and will swallow itself
and release the darkness
that will fill the chair again.
I shall be gone.
You will say you are here.
I can hear you say it.
I can almost hear you say it.
Soon you will take off your black coat
and the room's whiteness
will close around you
and you will move
to the back of the room.
Your name will no longer be known,
nor will mine.

I stand at the back
and you have just entered.
The beginning is about to occur.
The end is in sight.

The Story of Our Lives

To Howard Moss

1

We are reading the story of our lives
which takes place in a room.
The room looks out on a street.
There is no one there,
no sound of anything.
The trees are heavy with leaves,
the parked cars never move.
We keep turning the pages,
hoping for something,
something like mercy or change,
a black line that would bind us
or keep us apart.
The way it is, it would seem
the book of our lives is empty.
The furniture in the room is never shifted,
and the rugs become darker each time
our shadows pass over them.
It is almost as if the room were the world.
We sit beside each other on the couch,
reading about the couch.
We say it is ideal.
It is ideal.

2

We are reading the story of our lives
as though we were in it,
as though we had written it.
This comes up again and again.
In one of the chapters
I lean back and push the book aside

because the book says
it is what I am doing.
I lean back and begin to write about the book.
I write that I wish to move beyond the book,
beyond my life into another life.
I put the pen down.
The book says: *He put the pen down
and turned and watched her reading
the part about herself falling in love.*
The book is more accurate than we can imagine.
I lean back and watch you read
about the man across the street.
They built a house there,
and one day a man walked out of it.
You fell in love with him
because you knew that he would never visit you,
would never know you were waiting.
Night after night you would say
that he was like me.
I lean back and watch you grow older without me.
Sunlight falls on your silver hair.
The rugs, the furniture,
seem almost imaginary now.
She continued to read.
She seemed to consider his absence
of no special importance,
as someone on a perfect day will consider
the weather a failure
because it did not change his mind.
You narrow your eyes.
You have the impulse to close the book
which describes my resistance:
how when I lean back I imagine
my life without you, imagine moving
into another life, another book.
It describes your dependence on desire,
how the momentary disclosures
of purpose make you afraid.

The book describes much more than it should.
It wants to divide us.

3

This morning I woke and believed
there was no more to our lives
than the story of our lives.
When you disagreed, I pointed
to the place in the book where you disagreed.
You fell back to sleep and I began to read
those mysterious parts you used to guess at
while they were being written
and lose interest in after they became
part of the story.
In one of them cold dresses of moonlight
are draped over the chairs in a man's room.
He dreams of a woman whose dresses are lost,
who sits in a garden and waits.
She believes that love is a sacrifice.
The part describes her death
and she is never named,
which is one of the things
you could not stand about her.
A little later we learn
that the dreaming man lives
in the new house across the street.
This morning after you fell back to sleep
I began to turn pages early in the book:
it was like dreaming of childhood,
so much seemed to vanish,
so much seemed to come to life again.
I did not know what to do.
The book said: *In those moments it was his book.*
A bleak crown rested uneasily on his head.
He was the brief ruler of inner and outer discord,
anxious in his own kingdom.

4

Before you woke
I read another part that described your absence
and told how you sleep to reverse
the progress of your life.
I was touched by my own loneliness as I read,
knowing that what I feel is often the crude
and unsuccessful form of a story
that may never be told.
I read and was moved by a desire to offer myself
to the house of your sleep.
He wanted to see her naked and vulnerable,
to see her in the refuse, the discarded
plots of old dreams, the costumes and masks
of unattainable states.
It was as if he were drawn
irresistibly to failure.
It was hard to keep reading.
I was tired and wanted to give up.
The book seemed aware of this.
It hinted at changing the subject.
I waited for you to wake not knowing
how long I waited,
and it seemed that I was no longer reading.
I heard the wind passing
like a stream of sighs
and I heard the shiver of leaves
in the trees outside the window.
It would be in the book.
Everything would be there.
I looked at your face
and I read the eyes, the nose, the mouth . . .

5

If only there were a perfect moment in the book;
if only we could live in that moment,
we could begin the book again
as if we had not written it,
as if we were not in it.
But the dark approaches
to any page are too numerous
and the escapes are too narrow.
We read through the day.
Each page turning is like a candle
moving through the mind.
Each moment is like a hopeless cause.
If only we could stop reading.
He never wanted to read another book
and she kept staring into the street.
The cars were still there,
the deep shade of trees covered them.
The shades were drawn in the new house.
Maybe the man who lived there,
the man she loved, was reading
the story of another life.
She imagined a bare parlor,
a cold fireplace, a man sitting
writing a letter to a woman
who has sacrificed her life for love.
If there were a perfect moment in the book,
it would be the last.
The book never discusses the causes of love.
It claims confusion is a necessary good.
It never explains. It only reveals.

6

The day goes on.
We study what we remember.

We look into the mirror across the room.
We cannot bear to be alone.
The book goes on.
They became silent and did not know how to begin
the dialogue which was necessary.
It was words that created divisions in the first place,
that created loneliness.
They waited.
They would turn the pages, hoping
something would happen.
They would patch up their lives in secret:
each defeat forgiven because it could not be tested,
each pain rewarded because it was unreal.
They did nothing.

7

The book will not survive.
We are the living proof of that.
It is dark outside, in the room it is darker.
I hear your breathing.
You are asking me if I am tired,
if I want to keep reading.
Yes, I am tired.
Yes, I want to keep reading.
I say yes to everything.
You cannot hear me.
They sat beside each other on the couch.
They were the copies, the tired phantoms
of something they had been before.
The attitudes they took were jaded.
They stared into the book
and were horrified by their innocence,
their reluctance to give up.
They sat beside each other on the couch.
They were determined to accept the truth.

Whatever it was they would accept it.
The book would have to be written
and would have to be read.
They are the book and they are
nothing else.

The Untelling

He leaned forward over the paper
and for a long time saw nothing.
Then, slowly, the lake opened
like a white eye
and he was a child
playing with his cousins,
and there was a lawn
and a row of trees
that went to the water.
It was a warm afternoon in August
and there was a party
about to begin.
He leaned forward over the paper
and he wrote:

I waited with my cousins across the lake,
watching the grown-ups walking on the far side
along the bank shaded by elms. It was hot.
The sky was clear. My cousins and I stood
for hours among the heavy branches, watching
our parents, and it seemed as if nothing would enter
their lives to make them change, not even the man
running over the lawn, waving a sheet
of paper and shouting. They moved beyond the claims
of weather, beyond whatever news there was,
and did not see the dark begin to deepen
in the trees and bushes, and rise in the folds
of their own dresses and in the stiff white
of their own shirts. Waves of laughter carried
over the water where we, the children, were watching.
It was a scene that was not ours. We were
too far away, and soon we would leave.

He leaned back.
How could he know
the scene was not his?
The summer was with him,
the voices had returned and he saw the faces.
The day had started before the party;
it had rained in the morning
and suddenly cleared in time.
The hems of the dresses were wet.
The men's shoes glistened.
There was a cloud shaped like a hand
which kept lowering.
There was no way to know
why there were times that afternoon
the lawn seemed empty, or why even then
the voices of the grown-ups lingered there.
He took what he had written
and put it aside.
He sat down and began again:

We all went down to the lake, over the lawn,
walking, not saying a word. All the way
from the house, along the shade cast by the elms.
And the sun bore down, lifting the dampness, allowing
the lake to shine like a clear plate surrounded
by mist. We sat and stared at the water and then
lay down on the grass and slept. The air turned colder.
The wind shook the trees. We lay so long we imagined
a hand brushing the fallen leaves from our faces.
But it was not autumn, and some of us, the youngest,
got up and went to the other side of the lake
and stared at the men and women asleep; the men
in stiff white shirts, the women in pale dresses.
We watched all afternoon. And a man ran down
from the house, shouting, waving a sheet of paper.
And the sleepers rose as if nothing had happened,
as if the night had not begun to move
into the trees. We heard their laughter, then

their sighs. They lay back down, and the dark came over
the lawn and covered them. As far as we know
they are still there, their arms crossed over their chests,
their stiff clothing creased. We have never been back.

He looked at what he had written.
How far had he come?
And why had it grown dark just then?
And wasn't he alone when he watched the others
lie down on the lawn?
He stared out the window,
hoping the people at the lake,
the lake itself, would fade.
He wanted to move beyond his past.
He thought of the man
running over the lawn who seemed familiar.
He looked at what he had written
and wondered how he had crossed the lake,
and if his cousins went with him.
Had someone called?
Had someone waved goodbye?
What he had written told him nothing.
He put it away and began again:

I waited under the trees in front of the house,
thinking of nothing, watching the sunlight wash
over the roof. I heard nothing, felt
nothing, even when she appeared in a long
yellow dress, pointed white shoes, her hair
drawn back in a tight bun; even when
she took my hand and led me along the row
of tall trees toward the lake where the rest had gathered,
the men in their starched shirts, the women in
their summer dresses, the children watching the water.
Even then, my life seemed far away
as though it were waiting for me to discover it.
She held my hand and led me toward the water.
The hem of her dress was wet. She said nothing

when she left me with my cousins and joined
the others who stood together. I knew by the way
they talked that something would happen, that some of us,
the youngest, would go away that afternoon
and never find their way back. As I walked through the woods
to the other side of the lake, their voices faded
in the breaking of leaves and branches underfoot.
Though I walked away, I had no sense of going.
I sat and watched the scene across the lake,
I watched and did nothing. Small waves of laughter
carried over the water and then died down.
I was not moved. Even when the man
ran across the lawn, shouting, I did nothing.
It seemed as if the wind drew the dark
from the trees onto the grass. The adults stood
together. They would never leave that shore.
I watched the one in the yellow dress whose name
I had begun to forget and who waited with
the others and who stared at where I was
but could not see me. Already the full moon
had risen and dropped its white ashes on the lake.
And the woman and the others slowly began
to take off their clothes, and the mild rushes of wind
rinsed their skin, their pale bodies shone
briefly among the shadows until they lay
on the damp grass. And the children had all gone.
And that was all. And even then I felt
nothing. I knew that I would never see
the woman in the yellow dress again,
and that the scene by the lake would not be repeated,
and that that summer would be a place too distant
for me to find myself in again.
Although I have tried to return, I have always
ended here, where I am now. The lake
still exists, and so does the lawn, though the people
who slept there that afternoon have not been seen since.

It bothered him,
as if too much had been said.
He would have preferred
the lake without a story,
or no story and no lake.
His pursuit was a form of evasion:
the more he tried to uncover
the more there was to conceal
the less he understood.
If he kept it up,
he would lose everything.
He knew this
and remembered what he could—
always at a distance,
on the other side of the lake,
or across the lawn,
always vanishing, always there.
And the woman and the others would save him
and he would save them.
He put his hand on the paper.
He would write a letter for the man
running across the lawn.
He would say what he knew.
He rested his head in his arms and tried to sleep.
He knew that night had once come,
that something had once happened.
He wanted to know but not to know.
Maybe something had happened
one afternoon in August.
Maybe he was there or waiting to be there,
waiting to come running across a lawn
to a lake where people were staring
across the water.
He would come running
and be too late.
The people there would be asleep.
Their children would be watching them.

He would bring what he had written
and then would lie down with the others.
He would be the man
he had become, the man
who would run across the lawn.
He began again:

I sat in the house that looked down on the lake,
the lawn, the woods beside the lawn. I heard
the children near the shore, their voices lifted
where no memory of the place would reach.
I watched the women, the men in white, strolling
in the August heat. I shut the window
and saw them in the quiet glass, passing
each time farther away. The trees began
to darken and the children left. I saw
the distant water fade in the gray shade
of grass and underbrush across the lake.
I thought I saw the children sitting, watching
their parents in a slow parade along
the shore. The shapes among the trees kept changing.
It may have been one child I saw, its face.
It may have been my own face looking back.
I felt myself descend into the future.
I saw beyond the lawn, beyond the lake,
beyond the waiting dark, the end of summer,
the end of autumn, the icy air, the silence,
and then, again, the windowpane. I was
where I was, where I would be, and where I am.
I watched the men and women as the white
eye of the lake began to close and deepen
into blue, then into black. It was too late
for them to call the children. They lay on the grass
and the wind blew and shook the first leaves loose.
I wanted to tell them something. I saw myself
running, waving a sheet of paper, shouting,
telling them all that I had something to give them,
but when I got there, they were gone.

He looked up from the paper
and saw himself in the window.
It was an August night
and he was tired,
and the trees swayed
and the wind shook the window.
It was late.
It did not matter.
He would never catch up
with his past. His life
was slowing down.
It was going.
He could feel it,
could hear it in his speech.
It sounded like nothing,
yet he would pass it on.
And his children would live in it
and they would pass it on,
and it would always sound
like hope dying, like space opening,
like a lawn, or a lake,
or an afternoon.
And pain could not give it
the meaning it lacked;
there was no pain,
only disappearance.
Why had he begun in the first place?
He was tired,
and gave himself up to sleep,
and slept where he was,
and slept without dreaming,
so that when he woke
it seemed as if nothing had happened.
The lake opened like a white eye,
the elms rose over the lawn,
the sun over the elms.
It was as he remembered it—
the mist, the dark, the heat,

the woods on the other side.
He sat for a long time
and saw that they had come
and were on the lawn.
They were waiting for him,
staring up at the window.
The wind blew their hair
and they made no motion.
He was afraid to follow them.
He knew what would happen.
He knew the children would wander off,
that he would lie down with their parents.
And he was afraid.
When they turned
and walked down to the lake
into the shade cast by the elms
the children did wander off.
He saw them in the distance,
across the lake, and wondered if one
would come back someday
and be where he was now.
He saw the adults on the lawn,
beginning to lie down.
And he wanted to warn them,
to tell them what he knew.
He ran from the house down to the lake,
knowing that he would be late,
that he would be left
to continue.
When he got there,
they were gone,
and he was alone in the dark,
unable to speak.
He stood still.
He felt the world recede
into the clouds,
into the shelves of air.
He closed his eyes.

He thought of the lake,
the closets of weeds.
He thought of the moth asleep
in the dust of its wings,
of the bat hanging in the caves of trees.
He felt himself at that moment to be
more than his need to survive,
more than his losses,
because he was less than anything.
He swayed back and forth.
The silence was in him
and it rose like joy,
like the beginning.
When he opened his eyes,
the silence had spread, the sheets
of darkness seemed endless,
the sheets he held in his hand.
He turned and walked to the house.
He went to the room
that looked out on the lawn.
He sat and began to write:

THE UNTELLING

To the Woman in the Yellow Dress

FROM

The Late Hour

The Coming of Light

Even this late it happens:
the coming of love, the coming of light.
You wake and the candles are lit as if by themselves,
stars gather, dreams pour into your pillows,
sending up warm bouquets of air.
Even this late the bones of the body shine
and tomorrow's dust flares into breath.

Another Place

I walk
into what light
there is

not enough for blindness
or clear sight
of what is to come

yet I see
the water
the single boat
the man standing

he is not someone I know

this is another place
what light there is
spreads like a net
over nothing

what is to come
has come to this
before

this is the mirror
in which pain is asleep
this is the country
nobody visits

Lines for Winter

for Ros Krauss

Tell yourself
as it gets cold and gray falls from the air
that you will go on
walking, hearing
the same tune no matter where
you find yourself—
inside the dome of dark
or under the cracking white
of the moon's gaze in a valley of snow.
Tonight as it gets cold
tell yourself
what you know which is nothing
but the tune your bones play
as you keep going. And you will be able
for once to lie down under the small fire
of winter stars.
And if it happens that you cannot
go on or turn back
and you find yourself
where you will be at the end,
tell yourself
in that final flowing of cold through your limbs
that you love what you are.

My Son

(*after Carlos Drummond de Andrade*)

My son
my only son,
the one I never had,
would be a man today.

He moves
in the wind,
fleshless, nameless.
Sometimes

he comes
and leans his head,
lighter than air
against my shoulder

and I ask him,
Son,
where do you stay,
where do you hide?

And he answers me
with a cold breath,
You never noticed
though I called

and called
and keep on calling
from a place
beyond,

beyond love,
where nothing,
everything,
wants to be born.

White

for Harold Bloom

Now in the middle of my life
all things are white.
I walk under the trees,
the frayed leaves,
the wide net of noon,
and the day is white.
And my breath is white,
drifting over the patches
of grass and fields of ice
into the high circles of light.
As I walk, the darkness of
my steps is also white,
and my shadow blazes
under me. In all seasons
the silence where I find myself
and what I make of nothing are white,
the white of sorrow,
the white of death.
Even the night that calls
like a dark wish is white;
and in my sleep as I turn
in the weather of dreams
it is the white of my sheets
and the white shades of the moon
drawn over my floor
that save me for morning.
And out of my waking
the circle of light widens,
it fills with trees, houses,
stretches of ice.
It reaches out. It rings
the eye with white.
All things are one.
All things are joined
even beyond the edge of sight.

For Jessica, My Daughter

Tonight I walked,
close to the house,
and was afraid,
not of the winding course
that I have made of love and self
but of the dark and faraway.
I walked, hearing the wind
and feeling the cold,
but what I dwelled on
were the stars blazing
in the immense arc of sky.

Jessica, it is so much easier
to think of our lives,
as we move under the brief luster of leaves,
loving what we have,
than to think of how it is
such small beings as we
travel in the dark
with no visible way
or end in sight.

Yet there were times I remember
under the same sky
when the body's bones became light
and the wound of the skull
opened to receive
the cold rays of the cosmos,
and were, for an instant,
themselves the cosmos,
there were times when I could believe
we were the children of stars
and our words were made of the same

dust that flames in space,
times when I could feel in the lightness of breath
the weight of a whole day
come to rest.

But tonight
it is different.
Afraid of the dark
in which we drift or vanish altogether,
I imagine a light
that would not let us stray too far apart,
a secret moon or mirror,
a sheet of paper,
something you could carry
in the dark
when I am away.

From The Long Sad Party

Someone was saying
something about shadows covering the field, about
how things pass, how one sleeps towards morning
and the morning goes.

Someone was saying
how the wind dies down but comes back,
how shells are the coffins of wind
but the weather continues.

It was a long night
and someone said something about the moon shedding its white
on the cold field, that there was nothing ahead
but more of the same.

Someone mentioned
a city she had been in before the war, a room with two candles
against a wall, someone dancing, someone watching.
We began to believe

the night would not end.
Someone was saying the music was over and no one had noticed.
Then someone said something about the planets, about the
        stars,
how small they were, how far away.

The Late Hour

A man walks towards town,
a slack breeze smelling of earth
and the raw green of trees blows at his back.

He drags the weight of his passion as if nothing were over,
as if the woman, now curled in bed beside her lover,
still cared for him.

She is awake and stares at scars of light
trapped in the panes of glass.
He stands under her window, calling her name;

he calls all night and it makes no difference.
It will happen again, he will come back wherever she is.
Again he will stand outside and imagine

her eyes opening in the dark
and see her rise to the window and peer down.
Again she will lie awake beside her lover

and hear the voice from somewhere in the dark.
Again the late hour, the moon and stars,
the wounds of night that heal without sound,

again the luminous wind of morning that comes before the
     sun.
And, finally, without warning or desire,
the lonely and the feckless end.

Seven Days

FIRST DAY

I sat in a room that was almost dark,
looking out to sea. There was a light on the water
that release a rainbow which landed ne r the stairs.
I was surprised to discover you at the end of it.

SECOND DAY

I sat in a beach chair surrounded by tall grass
so that only the top of my hat showed.
The sky kept shifting but the sunlight stayed.
It was a glass pillar filled with bright dust, and you were inside.

THIRD DAY

A comet with two tails appeared. You were between them
with your arms outspread as if you were keeping the tails apart.
I wished you would speak but you didn't. I knew then
that you might remain silent forever.

FOURTH DAY

This evening in my room there was a pool of pink light
that floated on the wooden floor and I thought of the night
you sailed away. I closed my eyes and tried to think
of ways we might be reconciled; I could not think of one.

FIFTH DAY

A light appeared and I thought the dawn had come.
But the light was in the mirror and became brighter
the closer I moved. You were staring at me.
I watched you until morning but you never spoke.

SIXTH DAY

It was in the afternoon but I was sure
there was moonlight trapped under the plates.
You were standing outside the window, saying, "Lift them up."
When I lifted them up the sea was dark,
the wind was from the west, and you were gone.

SEVENTH DAY

I went for a walk late at night wondering whether
you would come back. The air was warm and the odor of roses
made me think of the day you appeared in my room,
in a pool of light. Soon the moon would rise
and I hoped you would come. In the meantime I thought
of the old stars falling and the ashes of one thing and another.
I knew that I would be scattered among them,
that the dream of light would continue without me,
for it was never my dream, it was yours. And it was clear
in the dark of the seventh night that my time would come soon.
I looked at the hill, I looked out over the calm water.
Already the moon was rising and you were here.

So You Say

It is all in the mind, you say, and has
nothing to do with happiness. The coming of cold,
the coming of heat, the mind has all the time in the world.
You take my arm and say something will happen,
something unusual for which we were always prepared,
like the sun arriving after a day in Asia,
like the moon departing after a night with us.

Snowfall

Watching snow cover the ground, cover itself,
cover everything that is not you, you see
it is the downward drift of light
upon the sound of air sweeping away the air,
it is the fall of moments into moments, the burial
of sleep, the down of winter, the negative of night.

An Old Man Awake in His Own Death

This is the place that was promised
when I went to sleep,
taken from me when I woke.

This is the place unknown to anyone,
where names of ships and stars
drift out of reach.

The mountains are not mountains anymore;
the sun is not the sun.
One tends to forget how it was;

I see myself, I see
the shine of darkness on my brow.
Once I was whole, once I was young . . .

As if it mattered now
and you could hear me
and the weather of this place would ever cease.

For Her

Let it be anywhere
on any night you wish,
in your room that is empty and dark

or down the street
or at those dim frontiers
you barely see, barely dream of.

You will not feel desire,
nothing will warn you,
no sudden wind, no stillness of air.

She will appear,
looking like someone you knew:
the friend who wasted her life,

the girl who sat under the palm tree.
Her bracelets will glitter,
becoming the lights

of a village you turned from years ago.

Exiles

Only they had escaped
to tell us how
the house had gone
and things had vanished,
how they lay in their beds
and were wakened by the wind
and saw the roof gone
and thought they were dreaming.
But the starry night
and the chill they felt were real.
And they looked around
and saw trees instead of walls.
When the sun rose
they saw nothing of their own.
Other houses were collapsing.
Other trees were falling.
They ran for the train
but the train had gone.
They ran to the river
but there were no boats.
They thought about us.
They would come here.
So they got to their feet
and started to run.
There were no birds.
The wind had died.
Their clothes were tattered
and fell to the ground.
So they ran
and covered themselves
with their hands
and shut their eyes

and imagined us
taking them in.
They could not hear
the sound of their footsteps.
They felt they were drifting.
All day they had run
and now could see nothing,
not even their hands.
Everything faded
around their voices
until only their voices were left,
telling the story.
And after the story,
their voices were gone.

2

They were not gone
and the story they told
was barely begun;
when the air was silent
and everything faded
it meant only that these
exiles came
into a country
not their own,
into a radiance
without hope.
Having come too far,
they were frightened back
into the night of their origin.
And on their way back
they heard the footsteps
and felt the warmth
of the clothes they thought
had been lifted from them.
They ran by the boats at anchor,

hulking in the bay,
by the train waiting
under the melting frost of stars.
Their sighs were mixed
with the sighs of the wind.
And when the moon rose,
they were still going back.
And when the trees
and houses reappeared,
they saw what they wanted:
the return of their story
to where it began.
They saw it in the cold
room under the roof
chilled by moonlight.
They lay in their beds
and the shadows of the giant trees
brushed darkly against the walls.

Pot Roast

I gaze upon the roast,
that is sliced and laid out
on my plate
and over it
I spoon the juices
of carrot and onion.
And for once I do not regret
the passage of time.

I sit by a window
that looks
on the soot-stained brick of buildings
and do not care that I see
no living thing—not a bird,
not a branch in bloom,
not a soul moving
in the rooms
behind the dark panes.
These days when there is little
to love or to praise
one could do worse
than yield
to the power of food.
So I bend

to inhale
the steam that rises
from my plate, and I think
of the first time
I tasted a roast
like this.
It was years ago
in Seabright,
Nova Scotia;

my mother leaned
over my dish and filled it
and when I finished
filled it again.
I remember the gravy,
its odor of garlic and celery,
and sopping it up
with pieces of bread.

And now
I taste it again.
The meat of memory.
The meat of no change.
I raise my fork
and I eat.

Poor North

It is cold, the snow is deep,
the wind beats around in its cage of trees,
clouds have the look of rags torn and soiled with use,
and starlings peck at the ice.
It is north, poor north. Nothing goes right.

The man of the house has gone to work,
selling chairs and sofas in a failing store.
His wife stays home and stares from the window into the trees,
trying to recall the life she lost, though it wasn't much.
White flowers of frost build up on the glass.

It is late in the day. Brants and Canada geese are asleep
on the waters of St. Margaret's Bay.
The man and his wife are out for a walk; see how they lean
into the wind; they turn up their collars
and the small puffs of their breath are carried away.

Where Are the Waters of Childhood?

See where the windows are boarded up,
where the gray siding shines in the sun and salt air
and the asphalt shingles on the roof have peeled or fallen off,
where tiers of oxeye daisies float on a sea of grass?
That's the place to begin.

Enter the kingdom of rot,
smell the damp plaster, step over the shattered glass,
the pockets of dust, the rags, the soiled remains of a mattress,
look at the rusted stove and sink, at the rectangular stain
on the wall where Winslow Homer's *Gulf Stream* hung.

Go to the room where your father and mother
would let themselves go in the drift and pitch of love,
and hear, if you can, the creak of their bed,
then go to the place where you hid.

Go to your room, to all the rooms whose cold, damp air you
        breathed,
to all the unwanted places where summer, fall, winter, spring,
seem the same unwanted season, where the trees you knew
        have died
and other trees have risen. Visit that other place
you barely recall, that other house half hidden.

See the two dogs burst into sight. When you leave,
they will cease, snuffed out in the glare of an earlier light.
Visit the neighbors down the block; he waters his lawn,
she sits on her porch, but not for long.
When you look again they are gone.

Keep going back, back to the field, flat and sealed in mist.
On the other side, a man and a woman are waiting;
they have come back, your mother before she was gray,
your father before he was white.

Now look at the North West Arm, how it glows a deep
　　cerulean blue.
See the light on the grass, the one leaf burning, the cloud
that flares. You're almost there, in a moment your parents
will disappear, leaving you under the light of a vanished star,
under the dark of a star newly born. Now is the time.

Now you invent the boat of your flesh and set it upon the waters
and drift in the gradual swell, in the laboring salt.
Now you look down. The waters of childhood are there.

The House in French Village

for Elizabeth Bishop

It stood by itself
in a sloping field,
it was white
with green
shutters and trim,

and its gambrel roof
gave it the look
of a small
prim barn.
From the porch

when the weather was clear,
I could see Fox Point,
across the bay
where the fishermen,
I was told,

laid out
their catch of tuna
on the pier
and hacked away with axes
at the bellies

of the giant fish.
I would stare
at Wedge Island
where gulls wheeled
in loud broken rings

above their young;
at Albert Hubley's shack
built over water, and sagging;
at Boutelier's wharf
loaded down

with barrels of brine
and nets to be mended.
I would sit
with my grandmother,
my aunt, and my mother,

the four of us rocking
on chairs, watching
the narrow dirt road
for a sign
of the black

baby Austin
my father would drive
to town and back.
But the weather
was not often clear

and all we could see
were sheets of cold rain
sweeping this way and that,
riffling the sea's coat
of deep green,

and the wind
beating the field flat,
sending up to the porch
gusts of salt spray
that carried

the odor of fish
and the rot,
so it seemed,
of the whole bay,
while we kept watch.

The Garden

for Robert Penn Warren

It shines in the garden,
in the white foliage of the chestnut tree,
in the brim of my father's hat
as he walks on the gravel.

In the garden suspended in time
my mother sits in a redwood chair;
light fills the sky,
the folds of her dress,
the roses tangled beside her.

And when my father bends
to whisper in her ear,
when they rise to leave
and the swallows dart
and the moon and stars
have drifted off together, it shines.

Even as you lean over this page,
late and alone, it shines; even now
in the moment before it disappears.

Night Piece

(after Dickens)

for Bill and Sandy Bailey

A fine bright moon and thousands of stars!
It is a still night, a very still night
and the stillness is everywhere.

Not only is it a still night
on deserted roads and hilltops
where the dim, quilted countryside seems to doze
as it fans out into clumps of trees dark and unbending
against the sky, with the gray dust of moonlight upon them,

not only is it a still night
in backyards overgrown with weeds, and in woods,
and by tracks where the rat sleeps under the garnet-crusted
    rock,
and in the abandoned station that reeks of mildew and urine,
and on the river where the oil slick rides the current
sparkling among islands and scattered weirs,

not only is it a still night
where the river winds through marshes and mudflats fouled
by bottles, tires and rusty cans, and where it narrows
through the sloping acres of higher ground covered with plots
cleared and graded for building,

not only is it a still night
wherever the river flows, where houses cluster in small towns,
but farther down where more and more bridges are reflected
    in it,

where wharves, cranes, warehouses, make it black and awful,
where it turns from those creaking shapes and mingles with
    the sea,

and not only is it a still night
at sea and on the pale glass of the beach
where the watcher stands upright in the mystery and motion
    of his life
and sees the silent ships move in from nowhere he has ever been,
crossing the path of light that he believes runs only to him,

but even in this stranger's wilderness of a city
it is a still night. Steeples and skyscrapers grow
more ethereal, rooftops crowded with towers and ducts
lose their ugliness under the shining of the urban moon;
street noises are fewer and are softened, and footsteps
on the sidewalks pass more quietly away.

In this place where the sound of sirens never ceases
and people move like a ghostly traffic from home to work and
    home,
and the poor in their tenements speak to their gods
and the rich do not hear them, every sound is merged,
this moonlit night, into a distant humming, as if
the city, finally, were singing itself to sleep.

New Poems

Shooting Whales

for Judith and Leon Major

When the shoals of plankton
swarmed into St. Margaret's Bay,
turning the beaches pink,
we saw from our place on the hill
the sperm whales feeding,
fouling the nets
in their play,
and breaching clean
so the humps of their backs
rose over the wide sea meadows.

Day after day
we waited inside
for the rotting plankton to disappear.
The smell stilled even the wind,
and the oxen looked stunned,
pulling hay on the slope
of our hill.
But the plankton kept coming in
and the whales would not go.

That's when the shooting began.
The fishermen got in their boats
and went after the whales,
and my father and uncle
and we children went, too.
The froth of our wake sank fast
in the wind-shaken water.

The whales surfaced close by.
Their foreheads were huge,
the doors of their faces were closed.
Before sounding, they lifted

their flukes into the air
and brought them down hard.
They beat the sea into foam,
and the path that they made
shone after them.

Though I did not see their eyes,
I imagined they were
like the eyes of mourning,
glazed with rheum,
watching us, sweeping along
under the darkening sheets of salt.

When we cut our engine and waited
for the whales to surface again,
the sun was setting,
turning the rock-strewn barrens a gaudy salmon.
A cold wind flailed at our skin.
When finally the sun went down
and it seemed like the whales had gone,
my uncle, no longer afraid,
shot aimlessly into the sky.

Three miles out
in the rolling dark
under the moon's astonished eyes,
our engine would not start
and we headed home in the dinghy.
And my father, hunched over the oars,
brought us in. I watched him,
rapt in his effort, rowing against the tide,
his blond hair glistening with salt.
I saw the slick spillage of moonlight
being blown over his shoulders,
and the sea and spindrift
suddenly silver.

He did not speak the entire way.

At midnight
when I went to bed,
I imagined the whales
moving beneath me,
sliding over the weed-covered hills of the deep;
they knew where I was;
they were luring me
downward and downward
into the murmurous
waters of sleep.

Nights in Hackett's Cove

Those nights lit by the moon and the moon's nimbus,
the bones of the wrecked pier rose crooked in air
and the sea wore a tarnished coat of silver.
The black pines waited. The cold air smelled
of fishheads rotting under the pier at low tide.
The moon kept shedding its silver clothes
over the bogs and pockets of bracken.
Those nights I would gaze at the bay road,
at the cottages clustered under the moon's immaculate stare,
nothing hinted that I would suffer so late
this turning away, this longing to be there.

A Morning

I have carried it with me each day: that morning I took
my uncle's boat from the brown water cove
and headed for Mosher Island.
Small waves splashed against the hull
and the hollow creek of oarlock and oar
rose into the woods of black pine crusted with lichen.
I moved like a dark star, drifting over the drowned
other half of the world until, by a distant prompting,
I looked over the gunwale and saw beneath the surface
a luminous room, a light-filled grave, saw for the first time
the one clear place given to us when we are alone.

My Mother on an Evening in Late Summer

1

When the moon appears
and a few wind-stricken barns stand out
in the low-domed hills
and shine with a light
that is veiled and dust-filled
and that floats upon the fields,
my mother, with her hair in a bun,
her face in shadow, and the smoke
from her cigarette coiling close
to the faint yellow sheen of her dress,
stands near the house
and watches the seepage of late light
down through the sedges,
the last gray islands of cloud
taken from view, and the wind
ruffling the moon's ash-colored coat
on the black bay.

2

Soon the house, with its shades drawn closed, will send
small carpets of lampglow
into the haze and the bay
will begin its loud heaving
and the pines, frayed finials
climbing the hill, will seem to graze
the dim cinders of heaven.
And my mother will stare into the starlanes,
the endless tunnels of nothing,
and as she gazes,
under the hour's spell,
she will think how we yield each night

to the soundless storms of decay
that tear at the folding flesh,
and she will not know
why she is here
or what she is prisoner of
if not the conditions of love that brought her to this.

3

My mother will go indoors
and the fields, the bare stones
will drift in peace, small creatures—
the mouse and the swift—will sleep
at opposite ends of the house.
Only the cricket will be up,
repeating its one shrill note
to the rotten boards of the porch,
to the rusted screens, to the air, to the rimless dark,
to the sea that keeps to itself.
Why should my mother awake?
The earth is not yet a garden
about to be turned. The stars
are not yet bells that ring
at night for the lost.
It is much too late.

Leopardi

The night is warm and clear and without wind.
The stone-white moon waits above the rooftops
and above the nearby river. Every street is still
and the corner lights shine down only upon the hunched
    shapes of cars.
You are asleep. And sleep gathers in your room
and nothing at this moment bothers you. Jules,
an old wound has opened and I feel the pain of it again.
While you sleep I have gone outside to pay my late respects
to the sky that seems so gentle
and to the world that is not and that says to me:
"I do not give you any hope. Not even hope."
Down the street there is the voice of a drunk
singing an unrecognizable song
and a car a few blocks off.
Things pass and leave no trace,
and tomorrow will come and the day after,
and whatever our ancestors knew time has taken away.
They are gone and their children are gone
and the great nations are gone.
And the armies are gone that sent clouds of dust and smoke
rolling across Europe. The world is still and we do not hear
    them.
Once when I was a boy, and the birthday I had waited for
was over, I lay on my bed, awake and miserable, and very
    late
that night the sound of someone's voice singing down a side
    street,
dying little by little into the distance,
wounded me, as this does now.

Mark Strand was born in Summerside, Prince Edward Island, Canada, and was raised and educated in the United States and South America. His most recent book of poems is *The Continous Life*, published in 1990. His book of short stories *Mr. and Mrs. Baby* was published in 1985. His translations include *The Owl's Insomnia*, a selection of Rafael Alberti's poems, and *Travelling in the Family*, a selection of Carlos Drummond de Andrade's poems, edited in collaboration with Thomas Colchie. He has written several children's books and edited several anthologies, including *Another Republic*, which he co-edited with Charles Simic. He has published numerous articles and essays on painting and photography, and in 1987 his book on William Bailey was published. He has been the recipient of fellowships from the Ingram Merrill, Rockefeller, and Guggenheim Foundations and from the National Endowment for the Arts. In 1979 he was awarded the Fellowship of the Academy of American Poets, and in 1987 he received a John D. and Catherine T. MacArthur Fellowship. He has taught at many colleges and universities, and since 1981 has been a professor of English at the University of Utah. In 1990 he was chosen by the Librarian of Congress to be Poet Laureate of the United States. He lives in Salt Lake City with his wife and son.

This book was set on the Linotype in a type face called Basker-ville. The face is a facsimile reproduction of types cast from molds made for John Baskerville (1706–1775) from his de-signs. The punches for the revived Linotype Baskerville were cut under the supervision of the English printer George W. Jones. John Baskerville's original face was one of the fore-runners of the type style known to printers as "modern face"— a "modern" of the period A.D. 1800.

Printed and bound by Halliday Lithographers,
West Hanover, Massachusetts